Unapologetic AF:
34 Ways to Unleash Your
Inner Badass

By:
Kelly Charles-Collins, Esq., MBA

Published By: Pen Legacy®

Cover By: Danielle A. Hercules

Library of Congress Cataloging – in- Publication Data has been applied for.

Paperback ISBN 978-1-7354880-1-1

eBook ISBN: 978-1-7354880-2-8

PRINTED IN THE UNITED STATES OF AMERICA.

Dedication

This book is dedicated to all the women who supported me, challenged me, uplifted me, hated on me, believed in me, looked up to me, mentored me, know me, coached me, ignored me, overlooked me, stood by me, stood up for me, loved me, saw me, see me, move me, and inspire me. It's also dedicated to those young girls and women who are me … in their own brilliantly beautiful way. I believe in you Sis. You got this!

"I belong everywhere I am, but I don't belong everywhere."
~ Kelly Charles-Collins

TABLE OF CONTENTS

Foreword

A late-night encounter on the new social audio app, Clubhouse, brought Kelly and me together — or rather a *chance* encounter. That night, our Clubhouse room was filled with lively discussions about becoming an author, leveraging your voice with podcasts, and just about anything online marketing. Kelly joined me and my co-moderators on stage to ask a question and mentioned that she was an author. I immediately sent her a message on Instagram asking if she had a podcast because, in my opinion, every author should have one. She did not, and in listening to her, I KNEW she had a voice and a story to share.

I invited Kelly to my *Launch Your Podcast* in a Weekend workshop, promising that her voice would be published to the world by the end of the weekend. Although skeptical, Kelly was up for the challenge.

During our podcast launch weekend, I could see the wheels turning in her head about how launching her podcast would leverage her voice and allow her "Ladies Who Leverage" network to have a voice, as well. You see, when you step into your power and your voice; you give others permission to do the same. That weekend, with the launch of the LWL podcast, the Ladies Who Leverage global movement was born.

I tell my students, "Launch your voice. Launch your brand. Do not seek to be a brand: Be a voice!"

We sometimes need someone outside of ourselves to see the big picture and connect all the moving parts in life. I saw Kelly's vision – a vision to hold space and create a global movement to give other women permission to be badass, step into their power, and leverage relationships and opportunities for good.

By the end of the weekend, we not only launched her LWL podcast, but we began her journey of leveraging her voice and the LWL brand to create influence and impact the world. This book is part of that journey. However, it's not just another book. Everything in this book reflects Kelly's life journey – her experiences and how she shows up in the world. Kelly embodies the spirit of a badass and is on a mission to empower women worldwide to do the same.

Kelly and I quickly became friends, and after launching her podcast, we realized her sister, Lisa Charles, was a dear friend and past coach of mine over a decade ago. After I received her sister's massive approval and trust, our work and deeper connection began.

I have two sayings: "Never stay where your presence is not valued" and "Always leave a presence when you are not present." Who would have thought that just a few months after our meeting on Clubhouse, I would be writing the foreword to Kelly's book? Yet, here we are, and as Kelly discusses in this book, that is a testament to the power of association, deep connections, and serving the right tribe.

Here's the thing; our time is now. The work begins by providing women with opportunities, resources, training, and the confidence to step into who they are and LEVEL UP.

Kelly has a unique gift for creating safe spaces for women to explore their hopes, dreams, and challenges without fear of judgment. Ladies Who Leverage consists of a group of women who all have one thing in common: the desire to unleash their badassery so they can live unapologetically AF. A former attorney, Kelly has permitted herself to change – to shapeshift into a leader versus an advisor and a spokesperson versus a taskmaster. I admire Kelly for her willingness to lead and allow others the opportunity to do the same. I know her story will inspire you, too.

Being a "badass" is taking opportunities presented, moving through fear, uplifting others, impacting people's lives, and living with purpose.

I remember one day, while getting a massage in Sedona, Arizona, the male massage therapist asked me, "Who are you waiting to rescue you? Don't you know you rescue yourself?"

I leave you with this: As we embark on this journey called life, there comes a time when we shed the past hurts, shed the tears, shed the victimhood, and become our own hero.

It's time to unleash your inner badass!

Be You! Be REAL! Be the Boss of Your Life!

HEATHER ANN HAVENWOOD
AWARD-WINNING MEDIA MOGUL
www.HeatherHavenwood.com

Preface

I am unapologetic AF (yes, as fuck).

But I didn't wake up like this. Unleashing my badassery takes work. Yes, "takes" in the present tense because it is part of my daily existence and I want it to be a part of yours.

That's why I wrote this book. Whether I'm with my Ladies Who Leverage Global Network or mentoring/advising women in my squad, I'm constantly sharing my Kellyisms – the principles that guide my life. As an award-winning TEDx speaker, author, mentor, and host of the Ladies Who Leverage podcast, these Kellyisms are not just cliché phrases. They are who I be (yes, I said be, not am) and how I live.

And yes, there's a backstory. There's always a backstory. I want you to know mine, so you have context for what you are about to experience in this book. What follows is probably not what book gurus call a "proper preface." But, oh well; It's my story and I've chosen to tell it my way. Give yourself grace and space to be you. That's what a badass does.

I hope it inspires you to unleash your inner badass too.

The Backstory

On October 22, 2019, I went to work in the downtown law firm where I was a partner. To me, it was just another Tuesday. When I arrived at work, I took a seat at my desk and began typing away, when suddenly I heard a voice. It wasn't a loud voice. It was a whisper but a noticeably clear whisper deep in my soul. "Turn around," the voice told me. So, I swiveled around in my chair, but there was nobody in the office except for me. As I sat there looking out in front of me, all I could see was the back wall of my office covered with my degrees and accomplishments. I sat there in silence, taking it all in. Feeling a sense of peacefulness come over me, out of nowhere, I uttered the words: "My freedom papers." Then I swiveled my chair back around and returned to typing as if nothing had happened.

A couple of hours later, I heard my phone beeping, alerting me to a call. It was one of my partners requesting me to come to his office. *Today is the day,* I thought to myself. I felt it in my soul. When I opened the door after walking to his office, there he sat at his desk, with the firm's managing partner sitting on the couch. I sat down in the chair near the desk and smiled as that same partner began to speak.

"Kelly, we want you to know that we enjoy working with you, and outside of the named partners, you are the best attorney in the firm. Now you know there are only two options after that. Either you're getting a promotion, or you're getting fired." He paused before continuing. "Kelly, as of the end of this year, you will no longer be employed here."

Yep, you read that right. They were firing me.

"Okay. I get it," I replied.

I wasn't surprised. I knew this day would come, either by their hand or mine. They just beat me to the punch.

I kept smiling as he continued talking.

"Kelly, we can no longer afford to pay you."

They had no idea how much truth was in that statement. It was not because they didn't have the money, but because I had been working on making myself priceless for the past thirty years.

At the age of sixteen, I graduated from high school and moved from Miami, Florida, to Providence, Rhode Island, to attend college. By the age of eighteen, I had passed all the tests to earn my associate's degree, and by age twenty, I received my bachelor's degree. You could say I was on my way to living what we have been led to believe is "the American Dream," which is to graduate from high school, go on to college, land a good job, then get married and have a family.

Know what other test I passed at age twenty? A pregnancy test. Was that the end of the dream? Well, it depends on how you view life.

I don't see life as linear. I believe to the depths of my soul that everything happens for a reason. Until age twenty, I had lived a good life – a carefree life. I had never really been challenged, but you know what they say: There's no better time than the present. For me, the present was in the summer of 1990. I was twenty years old, single, pregnant, and a couple of months from beginning my MBA program.

I had decisions to make. *Do I quit school? Do I end my pregnancy? Or do I let others speak shame and disappointment over my life?* I did none of those things. Instead, I chose to ignore any outside noise and stepped powerfully into who I was raised to be – the little girl born in Kingston, Jamaica, who was told she could be and do anything she put her mind to.

In the summer of 1990, I resolved to have my baby AND earn my MBA. I decided to live my life on my terms. I decided to create my own American Dream. I decided I could have it all and not let anybody tell me differently. I decided to show up for me because I knew I might have to show up for you one day.

Now, don't get me wrong. It wasn't easy. I was twenty-one years old with a baby, had two college degrees, and was about to start my MBA program. Also, even though I was working full-time, I was still part of the working poor, making only $340 a week. I couldn't pay rent, bills, *and* care for a baby on such a low income.

I applied for food stamps. They denied me. I applied for childcare assistance. They denied me. Why? Because they said I made too much money. Based on their income guidelines, *$340 a week was too much money!* Listen, that burned me to my soul. These people put a value on my worth, and I vowed I would never let that happen again.

Do you ever have that feeling? That feeling like someone else is in control of your destiny, and there's no way around it. It can make you feel like quitting, but quitting is not an option. I want you to know there is always a way. Yes, it may involve some losses and sacrifices, but loss and sacrifice are a part of life.

Back then, I was highly educated, motivated, and broke but not broken. At age twenty-one, I birthed my son into this world. I had no choice but to keep going. But there were days when I woke up and was overcome with the realization that I had somewhere to go, but because I couldn't afford a babysitter, my son didn't.

The first time it happened, it threw me. I had to go to work, but I had no friends or family to babysit, and I couldn't afford to pay a babysitter. I sat there thinking what was I going to do. I needed to go to work, but how could I do that if I had no one to care for my son in my absence. With no other choice, I decided to take him to work with me. I had no idea what my boss would think, but I got my son dressed, packed his diaper bag, and off to my job we went. When I got to my office, I gently placed him in his carrier under my desk like it was something I did every day. It took a while for my boss to realize he was there, but when she did, she acted like it was normal. At the end of my workday, I packed him up, drove to school, and gently placed him in his carrier on top of my desk. My professor wasn't as understanding as my boss, but I didn't care. It was just like that old song "my buddy, my buddy, Wherever I go, he goes."

That routine continued for a while, but things didn't get any easier. My pay remained the same, and it finally got to the point where I could no longer afford my car payments. So, I stopped paying for it. Chile, I even tried hiding my vehicle, but eventually, they found and repossessed it.

In hindsight, this all seems a little crazy and surreal. But that was my life, and I had to figure out a way *to make a way*. It was the beginning of me understanding my power.

I had no intention of letting anyone or anything get in my way. I was not going to allow external forces to stop me. You shouldn't either. I was a woman on a mission. Truthfully, at the time, I was just trying to survive. However, now, I fully understand that those bumps in the road were a necessary part of my journey. My mother says when you're born, your book is already written. I would like to add: you should feel free to edit accordingly. Through the power of clarity, intention, and purposeful action, I have done just that to my own book

My edited book led me on a journey to earning my MBA at age twenty-two while surviving on $340 a week and with a baby in tow.

It led me to power through law school in California, earning my law degree in two and a half years instead of three years, while leaving my son in Florida to be raised by my mother and sister.

It led me to start a wedding and event planning business because I still had bills to pay after losing a six-figure attorney job.

It led me to walk sixty miles in three days and start a 501(c)(3) nonprofit to raise money for breast cancer in honor of my mother.

It led me to become my son's momager and singing the hook on one of his songs, because that's what moms do!

It led me to accept a five-figure salary as an HR investigator after practicing law for thirteen years and not giving a damn about what anyone thought.

It led me to become a badass trial attorney who showed up and showed out every day because that's what I was supposed to do.

It led me to get the entire right side of my back tattooed because I felt like it.

It led me on the path of becoming an author and delivering a TEDx talk, both occurring in the same eleven-month period because I believed I could.

It led me to earn multiple six figures pursuing my purpose during a pandemic.

It led me to become the founder and CEO of the Ladies Who Leverage global movement because I want women to win.

But…

I'm not sharing these parts of my journey to boast. I share them because I want you to fully embrace that life is a journey – that your life is your journey. I want you to know that I've been there and experienced that. I want you to know that even if you've been there and experienced that, whatever that is, that you can still be and do anything you put your mind to. And you can be a badass while doing it!

Sometimes we allow pride, embarrassment, and others' opinions to get in our way. But who cares what they think? They only have the power you give them.

For example, at age forty-nine and having a multiple six-figure income, I was once again told I made too much money – this time by my partners who thought they had power over me.

Yes, it brought me full circle, but this time, it didn't burn my soul. Instead, it awakened the burning in my soul. That burning desire to unapologetically own my power. The grace to accept my *Freedom Papers* - The freedom I had prayed for, and the freedom to stand unapologetically in my greatness. The freedom to express what moves me. The freedom not to be questioned about my thoughts or to whom I allow access. The freedom not to have to look the other way. The freedom to be 100% me.

What made the difference? Time. Twenty-eight years to embrace what lies beneath.

ME!

I am a realist, and what I know is that you can't be anything to anyone until you're everything to yourself.

It took years of twists and turns, stops and starts, and accomplishments to unapologetically sit in my power, knowing that what lies beneath my success is ME.

This doesn't mean you travel this journey to success alone. Heck, I have invested in multiple coaches, mentors, and countless informal advisors. But no amount of coaching, mentoring, or advising matters if you don't first own your power.

For two years before I lost my last job, I was planning my exit. Some days I was all in on leaving and never going back. Other days, I retreated to the comfort of receiving bi-weekly paychecks. One foot in and one foot out. I had already spoken into the universe about my desire to leave my profession and pursue my purpose. It's funny, because the universe has a way of holding you to account. Losing my job was the push I needed and a stark reminder that my words and thoughts have power.

When that voice whispered to me to turn around so I could see the degrees and certificates hanging on the wall for all that I had accomplished and my soul spoke into existence those 3 words – my freedom papers – I knew without a doubt all would be well in my world. That's because I know that I belong everywhere I am, but I don't belong everywhere. That means I don't ever question why

I'm in a room. If I'm there, I belong there. But I also know that there comes a time in your life when your time has come; when through clarity and confidence, you know some people or places no longer deserve your presence; and when you understand that no matter the situation, you own your power.

On January 1, 2020, I was unemployed and had to decide whether I would continue playing footsie with my profession or step entirely into my purpose. Knocking on the door of fifty, I thought about my favorite poem, "The Dash" by Linda Ellis. The last line says, "So when your eulogy is being read, with your life's actions to rehash, would you be proud of the things they say about how you lived your dash?" This got me thinking about my legacy.

The choice was clear. Just like I did at 20, there would be no OR, it would be AND. I retired from practicing law after twenty-four years AND chose to go all in to leverage my profession to pursue my purpose.

I am now on a mission to create safe spaces for boss babe female entrepreneurs, enterprising side-hustlers, and corporate badasses, to collabosource so they can leverage their influence to create impact and income, own their power unapologetically AF, and live the life they've always envisioned. This book is one of those safe spaces and a piece of the legacy I want to leave behind.

But *Unapologetic AF* is not just a book; it's an experience. At the end of each Kellyism, I have included questions to help you reflect on and examine where you are on your journey to unleashing your inner badass.

So, don't waste another second. Here's what you need to do next:

1. Get your favorite pen and a highlighter
2. Grab your journal, ipad, phone, or whatever you use to take notes
3. Make your favorite beverage
4. Tell your family and friends you'll see them later
5. Find your favorite chair or lounging space
6. Dive into the book, savor every word and experience your transformation

And here's the best part … you don't have to experience this alone.

You already have a squad of badass women in the Ladies Who Leverage Global Network waiting to support you on your journey. *Go to www.LadiesWhoLeverage.com today and click "Join Now" to become an LWL Investor - the elite inner circle of the LWL Global Network.*

Also follow @LadiesWhoLeverage on Instagram and Facebook, share your unleashing journey on your social media, tag LWL and use the hashtags #unapologeticafbook, #ladieswholeverage, #unapologeti-caf, and #unleashyourinnerbadass.

Read at least the first 20 pages of the book and head over to Amazon and leave me a review. Go to www.KellysAmazon.com. I'd really appreciate it.

No more playing small.

It's time to unleash your inner badass and live life unapologetically AF!

Kelly

GET IT
TOGETHER
"Mindset is Everything"

1

Kellyism 1   **SEEK CLARITY**

Seeking clarity requires courage and vulnerability. It gives you peace of mind and provides direction. You must know where you are going or where you want to go, to figure out how to get there. There's no alignment without clarity. Clarity doesn't mean you have all the answers. Clarity, instead, makes the way for you to know what to ask and whom to ask those questions.

Clarity also equals cash. When you are clear about who you are, what you do, why you do it, how you do it, and who you do it for, it allows you to impact and influence others. As a result, income will follow.

REFLECTIONS

In what area of your life do you need to seek clarity? What actions will you take to get clear?

_____

_____

_____

_____

_____

_____

_____

_____

_____

_____

_____

_____

Kellyism 2

FIND YOUR PURPOSE

We often hear people talk about passion and purpose. I believe passion is a fleeting emotion – something that changes over time. On the other hand, I believe purpose is something more stable. It is your guiding light – the thing that drives and moves you. It is almost an innate characteristic. We might not realize our purpose until later in our lives, but you will likely see how your purpose has led you to who you have become once you know what it is. Some people refer to this as your "Ikigai," the Japanese term that loosely translates to "reason for being."

My purpose is to be the light for others to stand in their greatness. I am a safe space. I create safe spaces. My purpose is the core of who I am. It is my center. Your purpose is your center. It grounds you and keeps you in alignment.

REFLECTIONS

What is your life purpose?

_____

_____

_____

_____

_____

_____

_____

_____

_____

_____

_____

_____

_____

_____

_____

_____

_____

_____

_____

_____

_____

_____

_____

_____

_____

_____

_____

_____

_____

Kellyism 3

LIVE
INTENTIONALLY

E very year – around January 1ˢᵗ – we diligently list all the goals we want to accomplish in the new year. By mid-February, that list is a burden. Why? Because it is unrealistic. Tomorrow is not promised to you, much less next month or the next six months. So why begin the year by burdening yourself? Instead, make a "New *Day's* Resolution." Free yourself to live intentionally. Define your purpose. Identify what you want your life to look and feel like. Express gratitude for the good, bad, and ugly. Make a conscious decision to live life one day at a time on your terms. Then wake up every day and live!

REFLECTIONS

Today, what is your "New Day's Resolution?"

_____

_____

_____

_____

_____

_____

_____

_____

_____

_____

_____

_____

_____

_____

Kellyism 4

DITCH
THE LABELS

*N*ot good enough. Imposter syndrome. Hysterical. Emotional. Bossy. Too loud. Too aggressive. Too quiet. Too …

You get where I'm going. The negative stereotypes that have been attributed to women and that some of us have unfortunately embraced. Stop it! These labels don't belong to you. Do not claim them. Yes, it's as easy as that. You have the power to choose. Ditch the labels.

You are not a label.

You are the sum of your parts.

You are the axis of your universe.

You are each individual fraction of your being.

You are not other people's misperceptions.

You are exactly who you are meant to be.

You are uniquely you.

You are powerful.

You are a badass.

Labels are for packages. Ditch the labels!

REFLECTIONS

What labels have you assigned to yourself or have others assigned to you that you need to ditch?

_____

_____

_____

_____

_____

_____

_____

_____

_____

_____

_____

_____

_____

_____

_____

_____

_____

_____

_____

_____

_____

_____

_____

_____

_____

_____

_____

_____

Kellyism 5

PUT ON YOUR BIG GIRL PANTIES

There's no whining in badassery. Nobody is responsible for you but you. You can't expect people to want more for you than you want for yourself. Those who want you to win will show support, but nobody is going to drag you to your success. You must do the work. After all, your success is your responsibility, and personal responsibility requires you to take action. It's okay not to feel like it today. You don't have to hustle and grind twenty-four hours a day. Nor do you need to embrace hustle or grind as a strategy. You can work smarter, not harder. However, you must always have the desire and be willing to do what it takes to win. So, put on your big girl panties, and let's get it!

REFLECTIONS

What actions are you committed to take to ensure you win the game you have chosen to play?

_____

_____

_____

_____

_____

_____

_____

_____

_____

_____

_____

_____

_____

_____

_____

_____

_____

_____

_____

_____

_____

_____

_____

_____

_____

_____

_____

_____

_____

_____

_____

Kellyism 6

BELIEVE
IN YOURSELF

People do business and build relationships with people they know, like, and trust. That must begin with you. My dearly departed Aunt Kay once told me that you must love yourself more than you love anyone else. I didn't know what she meant at the time, but have now learned it over the years. You can't be anything to anyone until you're everything to yourself. You must know, like, and trust yourself first. You must believe in yourself. You are not an imposter.

We all have doubts and fears. The key is not to let your doubts and fears consume you or become your identity. You are enough. You are talented. Your voice is valuable. Your dreams matter. You are worthy. You are capable of everything you can imagine. If you don't believe in yourself, nobody else will. Your success begins and ends with you. You are a badass!

REFLECTIONS

List ten amazing things about you. Refer to this list whenever fear and doubt starts creeping in to rob you of your badassery.

_____

_____

_____

_____

_____

_____

_____

_____

_____

_____

_____

_____

_____

_____

_____

_____

_____

_____

_____

_____

_____

_____

_____

_____

_____

_____

_____

_____

_____

_____

_____

BOSS UP

"Stand in Your Power"

Kellyism 7   **SPEAK UP**

"When you see something, say something" should not just be another saying. It should be how you live your life. Don't be afraid to say what you mean and mean what you say. Speaking up for yourself and others is liberating. It's empowering. They say a closed mouth never gets fed. A closed mouth also relinquishes power. When we allow others to make decisions for us, we give away our power. When we defer to someone else to take action, we give away our power. When we fail to act when we know we should, we give away our power. Release any fears and doubts. Don't compromise your morals and values. We all have a voice. Use it. Speak truth to power. Silence is not an option!

REFLECTIONS

What was the last thing you spoke up about? Why did you speak up, and how did it make you feel? What do you need to speak up about?

_____

_____

_____

_____

_____

_____

_____

_____

_____

_____

_____

Kellyism 8

KNOW
YOUR VALUE

Value is not just about money. Before you even get to the money conversation, consider this – who do you believe yourself to be, and what do you feel you deserve in the world? This is where the value conversation begins. Be honest about the things that you believe about yourself and ask yourself, "Who said that about me? Why do I believe it?" Doing this reflection will help you understand these things are from outside sources that you have internalized and taken on as your own. This causes you to dim your light and diminish your value which impacts the way you show up in life.

You may have bumps and bruises, nicks, and scrapes. You may even be a "hot mess." Take comfort – the good, the bad, the ugly make us uniquely who we are. No matter your battle wounds, never relinquish or attribute your greatness to someone else. You have value. You determine your self-worth. Until you believe in yourself or believe that you deserve what you are asking for, you will never truly "know your value." So, repeat after me:

I AM ENOUGH. I AM WORTHY. I AM WHOLE.
I AM VALUABLE.

REFLECTIONS

Write down your self-worth affirmation. Repeat it three times every morning when you wake up and every night before you go to bed.

_____

_____

_____

_____

_____

_____

_____

_____

_____

_____

_____

_____

_____

_____

_____

_____

_____

_____

_____

_____

_____

_____

_____

_____

_____

_____

_____

_____

_____

_____

_____

Kellyism 9

NEGOTIATE
LIKE A BOSS

Negotiating like a boss requires you to know your value and not be afraid to demand it. But here's the secret. When negotiating, their number doesn't matter. Yes, I said it. Don't concern yourself with their number – only your numbers matter. Negotiation is an art and a skill. You must understand the strategy of *how* to negotiate. You must always be negotiating from a place of power. Before entering any negotiation, you must know your top number and your "walk away" number. You must also understand the value of those numbers. That means you know what you are willing to and not do for the negotiated rate. Your goal is to negotiate a deal that respects and aligns with your value. And if it doesn't, a boss must always be willing to walk away.

REFLECTIONS

What are your biggest challenges when it comes to negotiating?

_____

_____

_____

_____

_____

_____

_____

_____

_____

_____

_____

_____

_____

_____

_____

_____

_____

_____

_____

_____

_____

_____

_____

_____

_____

_____

_____

_____

_____

_____

Kellyism 10

GET YOUR MONEY

Nobody can ever pay you what you're truly worth. You're price-less. However, there is a value associated with the work you do, the services you provide, or the products you sell. Do not undervalue yourself. I'm often asked how I know what to charge. My response is: it's the number that makes you gag when you say it. If it rolls off your tongue too easily or if you tell someone and they don't hesitate, it's not high enough. The number should make them sit up and take notice. When you undervalue yourself, you're doing a disservice to yourself and those you serve. You must believe you are worth it. If you can't say it, they won't pay it. Demand what you want and be quiet. No explanation needed.

REFLECTIONS

When it comes to getting paid your worth, what holds you back?

_____

_____

_____

_____

_____

_____

_____

_____

_____

_____

_____

_____

_____

_____

_____

_____

_____

_____

_____

_____

_____

_____

_____

_____

_____

_____

_____

_____

_____

Kellyism 11

KNOW
YOUR ROLE

Have you ever been the only one or one of few and been asked to be the face or voice for a particular issue? Was your thought or response something like this, "I'm not your token or spokesperson You're not gonna use me for your PR stunt." If so, keep reading. Is that what they think of you or is that what you think of yourself. Do you think you're simply a token or spokesperson? Do you believe that makes you less than? Well, what if you reframed your thinking?

If you're the only one or one of few, why don't you think you're an expert? Why wasn't your first thought that you were selected because you and your life experiences make you uniquely qualified to speak to these issues? You are what you answer to, not what you're called or believe you're being called. The next time you're "the one," fix your crown, big up yuh chest (that's the Jamaican in me), and claim your title. You are an expert! Show up and answer to that.

REFLECTIONS

Think of a time when you were called upon to be the "one." How did you respond then? Why did you have that response? Would you respond differently now?

KNOW YOUR ROLE

Kellyism 12 OWN
YOUR POWER

We all have choices to make in life. Everything is one decision away. You have the power to choose whether shit happens to you or for you. You have the power to choose to not let others define your worth. You have the power to choose your definition of success and the path to get there. You have the power to choose who shares your life and journey. You have the power to choose to pursue your dreams or let them die a slow death because you have let others speak negativity and their own insecurities over your life. The decision is yours. Choose to unapologetically own your power!

REFLECTIONS

What decisions do you need to make to own your power unapologetically?

_____

_____

_____

_____

_____

_____

_____

_____

_____

_____

_____

_____

_____

_____

_____

_____

_____

_____

_____

_____

_____

_____

_____

_____

_____

_____

_____

_____

_____

_____

HOST A
BLOCK PARTY
"Set Your Boundaries"

Kellyism 13   **JUST SAY NO**

NO is a complete sentence and answer. For some reason, especially as women, we are reluctant to say NO. It feels as if we are rejecting the person instead of the request. We sometimes feel a sense of guilt or like we are being selfish. Let go of those thoughts and feelings. You have the right to say NO and without having to offer an explanation. Saying NO allows you to set boundaries for yourself and others. You cannot be anything to anyone until you are everything to yourself. Saying NO is one of the easiest forms of self-care. Saying NO is empowering. Saying NO to others is saying YES to yourself. And as Samuel Butler says, "Self-preservation is the first law of nature." So, just say NO!

REFLECTIONS

What or who do you need to say NO to and why haven't you done it yet?

_____

_____

_____

_____

_____

_____

_____

_____

_____

_____

_____

_____

_____

_____

_____

_____

_____

_____

_____

_____

_____

_____

_____

_____

_____

_____

_____

_____

Kellyism 14

PROTECT YOUR SPACE & PEACE

You must protect your space and peace to maintain your sanity. That might mean removing yourself from spaces or kicking people, including family, to the curb. It might involve saying no, not me, not today, not ever. Protecting your peace and space may also mean disappearing for a while from things like social media. Surround yourself with the right people. You are not obligated to keep anyone in your life. If they no longer serve you or are not in alignment with your journey, let them go. As my niece would say, it's time to observe "National Block a Bitch Day." You need people who nurture your soul and love you unconditionally, not those who thrive on drama and your destruction. Grace people who don't deserve your presence with your absence. You are the queen of your castle. Secure the doors.

REFLECTIONS

What boundaries do you need to establish to protect your space and peace?

_____

_____

_____

_____

_____

_____

_____

_____

_____

_____

_____

_____

_____

Kellyism 15

SHED DEAD WEIGHT

As we grow, everyone can't go! We will encounter different people throughout the stages of our life. We will have childhood and college friends, work colleagues, and community associates who become friends. Then, of course, we have our family. But not all these people can take the entire journey with you. It's true what they say; people are in your life for a reason or a season. As your priorities and values change or as you move from one socio-economic status to another, not everyone can go along this journey with you. They won't all understand your growth or be happy for you. Don't let that stop you. Let me also say that you might be the person you need to shed – all of those limiting beliefs and negative self-talk. And don't forget there might be places and things you might need to shed. But it's all good. Snakes shed their skin to allow further growth and remove parasites. You should do the same. And don't worry, shedding doesn't change you; it frees you. It's not personal; it's growth. Get to shedding.

REFLECTIONS

What or who do you need to shed? Why haven't you? When are you going to shed?

_____

_____

_____

_____

_____

_____

_____

_____

_____

_____

_____

_____

_____

_____

_____

_____

_____

_____

_____

_____

_____

_____

_____

_____

_____

_____

_____

_____

_____

_____

_____

_____

Kellyism 16 **CREATE YOUR LEGACY**

When people talk about building their legacy, they are usually referring to how much money they will be able to leave for their family when they die. But wealth is only one part of your legacy. Legacy is also about you – who you are and who you are being in this life. My favorite poem, *The Dash*, asks whether when you die, if you would be proud of the things people say about how you lived your life. How will you be remembered by those who loved you and encountered you? It's not enough to just nonchalantly move through life. You must live intentionally. Think about how you are showing up. How are you spending your time? What are you doing to impact lives around you? Do people's perceptions of you align with who you believe you are? How do you make people feel? Maya Angelou said, "people will forget what you said, they will forget what you did, but they will never forget how you made them feel." Your legacy is in your hands.

REFLECTIONS

What makes you proud about how you are living your life? What do you need to change?

_____

_____

_____

_____

_____

_____

_____

_____

_____

_____

_____

_____

_____

_____

_____

_____

_____

_____

_____

_____

_____

_____

_____

_____

_____

_____

_____

_____

_____

_____

_____

_____

BUCKLE UP

"You Got This"

Kellyism 17

TAKE THE
DETOUR

We've been taught the shortest distance between two points is a straight line. That might be true. However, the shortest distance is not always the right path. Many of us have been told to go to school, get a good job, then get married and have kids. But things don't always go as planned. Sometimes we need to take a left turn. Maybe even a U-turn. Perhaps we need to take a detour. Whatever the bump is, know that everything in life happens for a reason. You might not understand it at the time but trust the process. These bumps are a necessary part of your journey. They are the building blocks to your success. Life is not linear. Take the detour.

REFLECTIONS

What detours have you had to take and how has that impacted your life?

_____

_____

_____

_____

_____

_____

_____

_____

_____

_____

_____

_____

TAKE THE DETOUR

Kellyism 18

SIT
DON'T STAY

Celebrate your wins. Mourn your losses. In life, it's important for us to sit in the moment but don't stay there for long. Progress requires action. So, sit don't stay. We will all encounter failures and wins. When experiencing failure, or what I call a lesson, we want to wallow. We will rant, rave, and find someone to blame – whether ourselves or someone else. Misery loves company. Therefore, we tell everyone what happened and why it wasn't our fault.

On the flip side, when we have a win, we want to prolong our joy. We want to shout from the rooftops, bathe in the excitement, and not let the feeling go. However, sitting for too long in a feeling of disappointment or joy is counterproductive. I'm not saying for you not to acknowledge the pleasure or pain. Yes, take it all in so you will know what to do or what to avoid doing to replicate the feeling. But you can't sit and stay indefinitely in the feeling. By doing so, there's no forward progress. Get moving!

REFLECTIONS

What's the last accomplishment or lesson that caused you to sit? What motivated you to keep moving forward?

_____

_____

_____

_____

_____

_____

_____

_____

_____

_____

_____

_____

_____

_____

_____

_____

_____

_____

_____

_____

_____

_____

_____

_____

_____

_____

_____

_____

Kellyism 19 **ACCEPT YOUR
FREEDOM PAPERS**

I believe deep in my soul that everything happens for a reason. If you get fired, are overlooked for a promotion, don't close a deal, end a relationship, or whatever else you feel is a loss, take a deep breath, and accept your "Freedom Papers." Look at it as the chance to explore other opportunities. Loss of any kind is hard to deal with. But think of it as a clearing. An opening for something better to fill the void. If you lose your job, be clear that you have lost your job – not yourself. A job is what you do for a living, not who you are as a person. If you lose a relationship, that's okay too. You've lost that connection with that person, not your soul. If you didn't get "that promotion," there's a better one on the horizon. So, when someone or something is removed from your space, open your heart, mind and soul, and willingly accept your freedom papers. You'll thank me later.

REFLECTIONS

Journal about a time when you received your "Freedom Papers."
How did it make you feel and what lesson(s) did you learn?

_____

_____

_____

_____

_____

_____

_____

_____

_____

_____

_____

_____

_____

Kellyism 20

DO THE HARD THINGS FIRST

We have so many things we need to accomplish. Our to-do lists are often a mile long. We get overwhelmed trying to decide what to do first. The last thing we want is to end the day with few or none of the tasks completed. So, what do we do? We rush to complete the easy things because they don't take a lot of time and/or brainpower. Ahhh, the joy of checking a task off your list. But guess what's left? The hard things.

Let's face it; after having accomplished so much, you might be less inclined to tackle those things that are still left to do. Sure, there's always tomorrow and the day after that. But each day it goes uncompleted, it becomes a more daunting task.

The bottom line is that it still needs to get done. There's one guaranteed way to get it done, and that's by doing the hard things first. Completing the big tasks motivates you to keep going. Hard things first, easy things last. Tackling your to-do list in this way will result in you getting your tasks done in a day instead of several days, weeks, or months.

REFLECTIONS

What hard thing(s) do you need to prioritize to get done first?

_____

_____

_____

_____

_____

_____

_____

_____

_____

_____

_____

_____

_____

_____

_____

_____

_____

_____

_____

_____

_____

_____

_____

_____

_____

_____

_____

_____

_____

Kellyism 21   DO IT SCARED

Fear is a natural emotion. But often, we let it hold us back. Take a few minutes to think about the things that have been holding you back in life. What are the goals you want to pursue but don't because fear is getting in your way? Fear of failure. Fear of what other people might think. Fear of whether you can even achieve that goal.

Don't let fear stop you. Treat it like a hater and use it as your motivator. Nelson Mandela said, "Courage is not the absence of fear, but the triumph over it. The brave [person] is not [they] who does not feel afraid, but [they] who conquers that fear." Fear is a signal of something bigger and better on the horizon. Conquer your fears. Even if you feel you can't, just do it scared.

REFLECTIONS

What fear(s) do you need to conquer? What do you need to just do scared?

_____

_____

_____

_____

_____

_____

_____

_____

_____

_____

_____

_____
_____
_____
_____
_____
_____
_____
_____
_____
_____
_____
_____
_____
_____
_____
_____

Kellyism 22 **DO THE WORK**

Manifestation without action is a wish. We've all heard about vision boards. Perhaps you've even created one. If so, that's a great thing! But that's where it usually ends. Many of us have been led to believe the Law of Attraction will take care of the rest. Let's be real; things will not materialize with magical thinking alone. You also need to embrace the Law of Action. You need a plan. Start with designing your vision with my GRITTY Goals™ framework. Then take strategic action. No action = no results = no reward. Achieving your "GRITTY™ goals", requires you to do the work!

REFLECTIONS

What strategic actions do you need to take to achieve your GRITTY (Game-changing, Realistic, Intentional, Time-based, Tangible, Yearning) Goals™?

_____

_____

_____

_____

_____

_____

_____

_____

_____

_____

_____

_____

DO THE WORK

GET IN
FORMATION

"Play to Win"

Kellyism 23

LEVERAGE EVERYTHING

Leverage your expertise. Leverage your resources. Leverage your relationships. Leverage your voice. Leverage your personality. Leverage your humor. Leverage your quirks. Leverage your mistakes. Leverage your position. Leverage your privilege. Leverage your wins. Leverage your losses. Leverage your gifts. Leverage your time. Leverage your joy. Leverage your skills. Leverage your past. Leverage your present. Leverage your background. Leverage your potential. Leverage your superpower(s). Leverage every damn thing.

REFLECTIONS

What do you need to leverage to unleash your inner badass?

_____

_____

_____

_____

_____

_____

_____

_____

_____

_____

_____

_____

_____

_____

Kellyism 24

SECURE THE RIGHT SEAT

Not every seat is the right seat. We are so hung up on getting a "seat at the table" that some of us will sit any damn where. Your goal is to seek out the right seat at the right table. They will kick, scream, and even verbally express their objection, but they will still give some of us a seat. Don't fall into the trap of begging for or accepting just any seat. You are not window dressing, you're an expert. Don't sit in silence thankful that they let you in. Demand that your voice be heard. A heard, respected, and valued voice is empowerment. Be a valued contributor involved in decision-making that is integrated into the overall strategic plan. And always know that the right seat may be at the head of your own table.

REFLECTIONS

Before seeking your next right seat, ask yourself these questions:

1. Why do you want to be at that table?
2. What value do you bring to that table?
3. How does being at that table benefit you?
4. How does being at that table benefit the organization?
5. How will you use your voice at that table to benefit others?

_____

_____

_____

_____

_____

_____

_____

_____

_____

Kellyism 25   **GO BIG**

What game are you playing? And are you playing to win or simply not to lose? Living life unapologetically AF, gives you the freedom to execute the plays from your GRITTY™ goals playbook. And even if you stumble, loss and sacrifice are measures of life. So, risk being different. Risk being unique. Risk being joyful. Risk being the only one. Risk being the first one. Risk being hurt. Risk making mistakes. Risk having to sacrifice. Risk failure. Take the risk. Risk is part of your success journey. The biggest risk is the one you don't take. No risk. No reward. Go Big!

REFLECTIONS

In what area of your life do you need to "Go Big?"

_____

_____

_____

_____

_____

_____

_____

_____

_____

_____

_____

_____

_____

GO BIG

_____
_____
_____
_____
_____
_____
_____
_____
_____
_____
_____
_____
_____
_____
_____
_____
_____
_____
_____

Kellyism 26   **ASK**

Hoping, wishing, and praying will not cut it. People are not mind readers. Ask for what you want. Ask for what you need. Ask for help. Don't let pride block your blessings. Sometimes it's better to take action and ask for forgiveness later than delay action to seek approval. Ask for forgiveness not permission. The only dumb question is the one you don't ask. They say, "ask and you shall receive." So, ask.

REFLECTIONS

What do you need to ask for?

_____

_____

_____

_____

_____

_____

_____

_____

_____

_____

_____

_____

_____

_____

_____

Kellyism 27   **BUILD YOUR SQUAD**

Everybody needs a squad – those true ride-or-die individuals who will be there to celebrate the good and mourn the bad with you. Those who will love you and check you when you're wrong. Your squad should not consist of "yes" women. Your squad is not your competition. Your squad is those people in your corner who will build you up, inspire you, push you, and hold you accountable. You trust your squad, and they trust you. You are all on the same mission, even if you have a different vision. A true squad makes sure nobody gets left behind. Like Oprah said, "Your squad will ride with you on the bus when your limo breaks down."

Let's be real, though. Some of your squad will come organically, while there are others that you'll need to be resourceful to connect with and even some who you will need to pay to gain access to them. That's just how it goes. You must be willing to invest time, energy, and money to build the right squad of advisors, coaches, mentors, and sponsors. There's power in association, and proximity is power. Get to building!

REFLECTIONS

Who's in your squad, and who needs to be in your squad?

_____

_____

_____

_____

_____

_____

_____

_____

_____

_____

_____

_____

_____

_____

_____

_____

_____

_____

_____

_____

_____

_____

_____

_____

_____

_____

_____

_____

_____

_____

Kellyism 28   **COLLABOSOURCE**

The secret sauce of the Ladies Who Leverage Global Network is "collabosourcing.®" Being a female entrepreneur or a corporate professional is not easy, and your relationships are everything. But building networks can be daunting. Your squad, circle, village, peeps, girls, sisters, whatever you call them, are your network. That's why in Ladies Who Leverage, we don't compete, we collabosource. Collabosourcing® is leveraging your expertise, resources, and relationships to build your business, brand, and badassery. If you are committed to leveraging your influence to create impact and increase your income, build your net worth by leveraging your network.

REFLECTIONS

How would having a squad to collabosource with change your life? Pro tip: Join Ladies Who Leverage to find out.

_____

_____

_____

_____

_____

_____

_____

_____

_____

_____

_____

_____

_____

_____

_____

_____

_____

_____

_____

_____

_____

_____

_____

_____

_____

_____

_____

_____

Kellyism 29

LISTEN, LEVERAGE, IMPLEMENT

We love going to conferences, webinars, workshops, coaching sessions, group meetings, etc. But what do you do with all the information you learn? Are you a "gem" hoarder? Do you have an app or notebook filled with all the dazzling "gems" you've learned, but don't implement? You're not alone. While at these events, we listen intently, get excited, and have our souls set on fire. We often proclaim, "YAASSS! I can't wait for this to be over so I can get to work." But let's tell the truth and shame the devil. For many of us, those notes become a graveyard of unused information. If you're guilty of such, let's change that.

Focus on the top three to five gems aligned with your goals and what you can leverage to grow in your business or career. Circle, highlight, place a star beside them – whatever you need to do to highlight those gems. Give those gems a place of honor where they will get the required attention. Next, set an implementation date. Reverse engineer to determine what expertise, resources, and relationships you need to implement those gems. Then do it. Listen. Leverage. Implement. Easy as 1-2-3.

REFLECTIONS

List three to five gems you have learned from this book that you
need to implement.

_____

_____

_____

_____

_____

_____

_____

_____

_____

_____

_____

_____

_____

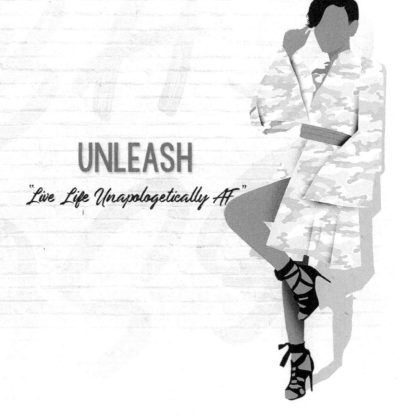

UNLEASH

"Live Life Unapologetically AF"

Kellyism 30 **TWIRL ON
YOUR HATERS**

You better buckle up because "they" will come for you. "They" can be anyone – family, friends, colleagues, business partners, or strangers. Not everyone in your life will celebrate you, and not everyone is going to believe in you. Not all of them are just going to go quietly in the night and mind their business. They will come for you publicly. They will try to undermine you, break you, and destroy you. You cannot let them win. You must steel yourself in knowing you are a badass. Know that you belong everywhere you are. Know that what they think about you is not your business and is not a reflection of you but their shortcomings and fears. "Know the difference between those who stay to feed the soil and those who come to grab the fruit." (Author Unknown) Buckle up to protect yourself from the haters. Because we already know; haters are gonna hate, and that's just life. Ignore the noise and twirl on those haters.

REFLECTIONS

Celebrate a time you twirled on your haters.

_____

_____

_____

_____

_____

_____

_____

_____

_____

_____

_____

_____

_____

_____

_____
_____
_____
_____
_____
_____
_____
_____
_____
_____
_____
_____
_____
_____
_____
_____
_____
_____

Kellyism 31   **JUST BE YOU**

There's a saying that "comparison is the thief of joy." I couldn't agree more. Too often, we go through life comparing ourselves to the "thems" and "theys" of the world. You can never be them Sis, nor should you want to be. So, stop trying! You are uniquely made. You are uniquely suited and were specifically chosen for your role in this world. Spending time trying to be someone else is a waste of your energy and brilliance. Focus on you. Focus on your gifts. Who do you want to be in this world? What impact do you want to make? What will be your legacy? You only have this one life to live. Live yours not anybody else's.

REFLECTIONS

Whose life have you been trying to live? What are you going to do to live *your life* unapologetically AF?

_____

_____

_____

_____

_____

_____

_____

_____

_____

_____

_____

_____

_____

_____

_____

_____

_____

_____

_____

_____

_____

_____

_____

_____

_____

_____

_____

_____

_____

_____

Kellyism 32

DARE TO BE DIFFERENT

Why should you dare to be different? Because Sally Hogshead says, "Different is better than better," and she's right. We're always striving to be better. It's what we have been taught. Most people's goals are to get a better house, car, education, job, relationship, you name it. We feel we must be better, but trying to be "better" is a never-ending chase. There's always someone or something better. Being better requires you to compare yourself to others, but as we know, comparison is the thief of joy. Reject the pressure to conform. Dare to shake shit up. Dare to be unique. Dare to ask questions. Dare to push boundaries. Dare to do it your way. Dare to stand out. Dare to go against the grain. Dare to be a trailblazer. Dare to own your power unapologetically. Just do it and be different while doing it!

REFLECTIONS

How will you dare to be different?

_____

_____

_____

_____

_____

_____

_____

_____

_____

_____

_____

_____

_____

_____

_____

_____

_____

_____

_____

_____

_____

_____

_____

_____

_____

_____

_____

_____

Kellyism 33   BE A BADASS

Badasses come in all shapes, sizes, colors, professions, etc. But here are some of their common traits:

- Self-confidence, resilience, persistence, and perseverance
- Learner, teacher, listener, and discoverer
- Collabosourcer
- Empowers other women
- Unapologetically owns her power
- Knows she belongs everywhere she is and doesn't belong everywhere
- Lives the life she envisions
- Demands her worth
- Says NO without explanation

REFLECTIONS

What makes you a Badass? What are some other traits of a badass?

_____

_____

_____

_____

_____

_____

_____

_____

_____

_____

_____

_____

_____

Kellyism 34   UNLEASH YOUR BADASSERY

It's time! Time to unleash your inner badass. So, show up, and as my stylist, Michele Lopez, says, "be intentional." Do not allow the people of the world to dictate how you operate in life. So often, we hide and shrink. We dim our light because we think it's shining too bright in other's eyes. That shouldn't be your concern. Let them wear shades.

I tell all the women in my Ladies Who Leverage Global Network, *"unleash your badassery!"* This is one of my favorite Kellyisms; it means you must show up and show out every single day. Overcome your fears and show up. This is something I must keep reminding myself. I know you don't always feel like it, but do it anyway. There are also times when I don't talk about my accomplishments or put things out into the world for others to see. That's because I was raised not to brag or boast. Know that you are great and celebrate your accomplishments. "It ain't bragging if it's true." You need to give all your authentic self to the world.

When unleashing your badassery becomes the norm for you, you will show up and show out no matter what's happening in your life. As a badass, the end goal is to always make your presence felt.

REFLECTIONS

Which of these thirty-four ways will you implement to unleash your inner badass?

_____

_____

_____

_____

_____

_____

_____

_____

_____

_____

_____

_____

_____

_____

_____

_____

_____

_____

_____

_____

_____

_____

_____

_____

_____

_____

_____

_____

_____

_____

_____

Congratulations on taking the first step to unleashing your inner badass!

But that's only the beginning. If you are ready to:

- Be held accountable
- Collabosource with a diverse group of badass women to broaden your network and build authentic, strategic relationships
- Get clarity and experience transformational breakthroughs
- Become a CEO who works on your business not in your business
- Accelerate your business & career growth
- Openly share your expertise, resources, and relationships
- Leverage your influence to create impact and income
- Live life unapologetically AF

Go to www.LadiesWhoLeverage.com today and click "Join Now" to become a Ladies Who Leverage Investor – the elite inner circle of the LWL Global Network.

More about Ladies Who Leverage:

Mission: Ladies Who Leverage is a global network of women who collabosource to leverage their influence to create impact and increase their income so they can live life unapologetically AF.

Collabosourcing®: Leveraging your expertise, resources, and relationships to build your business, brand, and badassery.

Vision: Become the global leader for female entrepreneurs, side-hustlers and corporate professionals who are committed to building trusted relationships, creating community, and leveraging their influence to positively impact the world and create income.

Environment: LWL is a safe, professional network where women can share and explore their hopes, dreams, and fears without judgment or fear of competition.

Our Motto: We don't compete. We collabosource.

Social Responsibility: We are committed to empowering girls and young women through charitable endeavors and collaborative partnerships. We believe that we have a responsibility to model what is possible and provide opportunities for exposure, education, and empowerment.

Bedrock Principles:

- Collabosource
- Strategize
- Monetize

Core Values:

- Collabosouring
- Empowerment
- Respect
- Integrity
- Commitment
- Service
- Accountability
- Fun
- Freedom
- Vision

Connect with the Ladies Who Leverage Global Network. *It's a Movement!*

Website: www.ladieswholeverage.com

Facebook: www.facebook.com/ladieswholeverage

Facebook: www.facebook.com/groups/ladieswholeverage

Instagram: www.instagram.com/ladieswholeverage

Podcast: www.ladieswholeveragepodcast.com

LinkedIn: www.linkedin.com/in/ladieswholeverage

LinkedIn: www.linkedin.com/in/ladieswholeveragepodcast

Email: info@ladieswholeverage.com

ABOUT THE AUTHOR

Kelly **Charles-Collins** is a badass CEO, trial attorney, TEDx speaker, author, and podcast host.

Kelly and her award-winning TEDx Talk - *The Bystander Effect: Why Some People Act and Others Don't* have been featured on television and other media, and she's been quoted in several publications, including ABC, NBC, Forbes, and Fast Company.

Kelly's unique ability to make difficult and sensitive topics more approachable has allowed her to leverage her 20+ years of employment law experience, intuitive perspective, and engaging personality, to empower leaders to stay on the right side of the next #hashtag movement.

She is an expert on disrupting unconscious bias, bystander intervention, and engaging in courageous conversations and is the author of:

- *ACE Your Workplace Investigations*
- *Speak: Silence is Not an Option! and*
- *Conversations Change Things: The "PER"fect Framework for Courageous Conversations.*

In March 2020, Kelly founded the Ladies Who Leverage Global Network and in 2021, launched the Ladies Who Leverage Podcast to support boss babe female entrepreneurs, enterprising side-hustlers, and corporate badasses to succeed in their business and career. Kelly is on a mission to create safe spaces for women to collabosource so they can leverage their influence to create impact and income, own their power unapologetically AF, and live the life they've always envisioned.

Connect with Kelly:

www.ladieswholeverage.com
www.kellycharlescollins.com
www.ladieswholeveragepodcast.com
IG & Facebook: Ladies Who Leverage
Clubhouse: KellyCCollins
LinkedIn: www.linkedin.com/in/kellycharlescollins

Made in the USA
Columbia, SC
11 November 2021

48714518R00098